YOUR FIRST

Horse Book

Peter R. Winkelaar

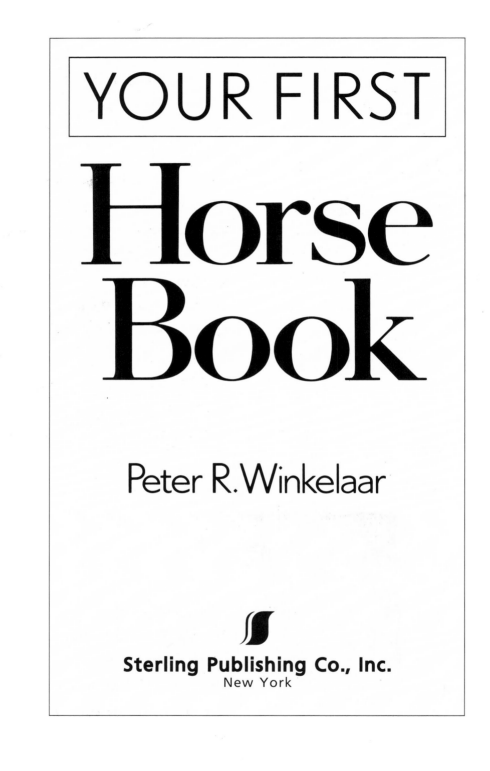

Sterling Publishing Co., Inc.
New York

Translated by Fay Greenbaum
Edited by Claire Bazinet

Library of Congress Cataloging–in–Publication Data

Winkelaar, Peter R.
   [Premier livre sur les chevaux pour les jeunes. English]
   Your first horse book / by Peter R. Winkelaar ; [translated by Fay Greenbaum].
      p.   cm.
   Includes index.
   Summary: Discusses different breeds of horses and how to ride and care for them.
   ISBN 0-8069-9525-4
   1. Horses–Juvenile literature.   2. Horsemanship–Juvenile literature.   [1. Horses.   2. Horsemanship.]
   I. Title.
   SF302.W5413   1996
   636.1–dc20   96–18326
                                                CIP
                                                AC

VK

10 9 8 7 6 5 4 3 2 1

Published by Sterling Publishing Company, Inc.
387 Park Avenue South, New York, N.Y. 10016
Originally published by Le Ballon N.V. Antwerp, Belgium
under the title *Premier livre sur les chevaux pour les jeunes*
©·1995 by De Ballon
English translation © 1996 by Sterling Publishing Co., Inc.
Distributed in Canada by Sterling Publishing
   ℅ Canadian Manda Group, One Atlantic Avenue,
   Suite 105, Toronto, Ontario, Canada M6K 3E7
Distributed in Great Britain and Europe by
   Cassell PLC, Wellington House, 125 Strand,
   London WC2R 0BB, England
Distributed in Australia by
   Capricorn Link (Australia) Pty Ltd.
   P.O. Box 6651, Baulkham Hills,
   Business Centre,
   NSW 2153, Australia
Printed in Italy
All rights reserved

Sterling ISBN 0-8069-9525-4

Contents

Understanding Horses

The horse, an animal with remarkably developed senses of hearing, smell, and sight, is always ready to gallop off in an instant. His ears can pick up the faintest of distant noises, and his eyes, positioned at the sides of his head, allow him to see a wide

area around him. Because the horse cannot look directly backwards, it is risky to pass close behind him unexpectedly. If he feels threatened, he will react quickly to defend himself.

A horse cannot move his eyes up and down as we can. To make out a distant object, he raises his head. The horse's sense of smell, one of his most important senses, is comparable to that of a hunting dog's. When traveling over uneven ground, it's often best to allow the horse to pick his own way; he will instinctively find the best path. If your horse categorically refuses to go where you want him to, it's most likely that he senses something wrong. Some riders, however, don't trust

their horse's instincts and, because they don't understand these natural talents, they punish him. It is important to learn why horses act as they do, and your own horse's individual characteristics, for the best of relationships.

Above left: Horses sniff each other to recognize friends and learn about newcomers. It's possible that their sharp sense of smell allows them to recognize fear from a rider's perspiration.

Above right: To understand horses, watch how they behave towards each other, such as when a colt joins a herd or as he grows up. Through testing behavior, horses learn the extent of their power and how they fit in with the others in the group.

Left: In the herd, the colt quickly learns to play "Who is strongest?" The game allows him to measure himself physically against others without getting hurt.

Left above: Horses take flight at any threat of danger, assuring their safety in nature. *Middle left*: When alert, a horse's ears are positioned forward. *Middle right*: If anxious or aggressive, the horse lays the ears back towards his neck. *Far right*: A horse that pulls the upper lip back, in a sort of smile, is smelling a very strong odor.

THE EARS

Horses can move their ears in all directions. In addition to their excellent hearing, they have a very good memory for sounds. The tone of a rider's voice is how the horse recognizes praise or punishment.

THE EYES

A horse's eyes can move from side to side, but not up or down.

THE HEAD

The horse can easily hold the head up, stretch it forward, let it hang, or make rocking motions side to side.

THE NOSE

To horses, smell is the key to under-standing the world around them. The sense is far more developed than in the human nose.

Outward display of the horse's mood

Horses express how they feel through their behavior. An animal whose neck is forcefully extended, with the head stretched upward, is in an aggressive mood, while one who lays back his ears, opens his eyes wide, swishes his tail, and steps around nervously feels threatened. Lifting the head with the ears pointed, the tail raised, and the nostrils flaring, wide open, is a sign of excitement in a horse. A horse that is agitated, in a sweat, with eyes bulging is suffering and likely in pain. A satisfied horse will act calmly and have a friendly, approachable look, with only a quiet movement of the tail.

Odors provide a horse with all kinds of information; coming upon a stranger's manure, for example, a horse can tell if the animal is a stallion or mare, or if it comes from a stable or pasture.

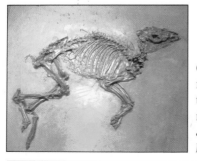

From Wild Horse to Saddle Horse

One of the oldest fossils found of a distant ancestor of the horse. It dates from the middle of the Eocene period and was discovered near Messel, in Germany.

Eohippus, the ancestor of our modern horse, lived 55 million years ago. This horse of long ago galloped across what is now the American continent. After passage of about a million years, Eohippus grew larger. The name changed to Mesohippus and, later still, to Merychippus. Then Pliohippus appeared, the first horse with a single, unified

Eohippus
lived 55 million years ago. Height only about 10 inches (25 cm)

Mesohippus
lived 25 to 40 million years ago. Size: 23½ inches (60 cm)

Merychippus
measured about 39 inches (100 cm) at the withers.

Pliohippus
gradually left the woods for the prairie. Size: 49 inches (125 cm)

Equus the ancestor of all horses. Its height at the withers varies.

A drawing of ponies on a wall in the cave at Lascaux. The brown and white colors were applied with a little piece of straw. One of the ponies is drawn pierced by arrows, a sign of a successful hunt.

The Przewalski horse, discovered in 1881, is on the protected animals list. There are only a few hundred left, in American and European zoos, where their breeding and reproduction are a matter of great concern. Przewalski horse is the last of the wild horse breeds.

hoof. Finally came Equus, which divided into three basic horse groups: the Przewalski breed, and the tarpans of the steppes and of the forests, both of which are now extinct.

Mankind first encountered the horse about 30,000 years ago. This we know from the cave drawings found at Lascaux in France. Clay tablets engraved around 4,000 years ago tell us that it was nomads who first tamed horses. At the time, the animals were kept as livestock and their skin was used to make tents and clothing, while their dried excrement served as fuel. Gradually, the strength of the horse was recognized and certain types were selected to carry or pull burdens. Little by little, the importance of the horse grew in the eyes of their human caretakers. Some tribal chiefs even arranged to have their mounts buried with them. For combat, warriors selected and rode horses that were bigger and faster than others. The Assyrians, famous for their horsemanship,

rode seated on blankets or cushions; the early wooden–frame saddle did not come into use until much later. In the Middle Ages, increasing danger from the bow and arrow made heavy defensive equipment necessary. By the Renaissance, the fashion of the knight in armor faded. What survived were the traditional movements of combat horsemanship: jumping, reverse turns, and rearing. Across Europe, riding schools opened to teach these techniques, but the development of modern weapons soon ended the use of the all too vulnerable horse in combat.

Right: Vienna's Spanish Riding School is the oldest school of classical equestrian art in the world, a style of horsemanship that is still taught today. It was in 1729 that an architect, Fischer von Erlach, received a commission from Emperor Charles VI to build a home for the Imperial Spanish Riding School. At that time, Spanish horses, which came from Arabian stallions, were very popular with the nobility. In 1580, the emperor's stud farm was located at Lipica; where the horses destined to be used at court were bred. The colts were called Lipizzaners. Ever since, these are the only horses used and trained by the Spanish Riding School.

People discovered that, in times of war, horses were of much help in pulling carriages. Later they realized that, mounted on horseback, soldiers would occupy a position of strength.

As the muscular power of the horse became recognized, certain types were chosen for their ability to carry or pull heavy burdens. The earliest such chore was likely dragging a log along the ground.

The North American cowboys and the gauchos of Argentina use calm and cooperative working horses to drive herds of cattle to pasture.

Pony Breeds

ISLAND PONY

A solid pony with an excellent sense of direction, its size varies from about 12 to 14 hands. Its coat can be of any color, even black or chestnut. This pony is used for riding and also as a pack animal.

HAFLINGER

This breed of pony is able to carry heavy loads on steep slopes, like those of its alpine homeland. Its gentleness and character make it a good saddle horse for children. Coat is chestnut. Size: $13\frac{1}{4}$ to $14\frac{1}{4}$ hands.

NORWEGIAN OR FJORD PONY

The Fjord pony, an ancient breed, is dun with dark points. Its mane is cut to look like a brush. It is used for work in forestry and agriculture, as well as for recreation. Size: 13 to $14\frac{1}{2}$ hands.

SHETLAND PONY

This robust and ancient breed is particularly suitable for children. Despite their being sometimes skittish, the Shetland basically has a good character. Modest in size, only $9\frac{1}{2}$ hands, these hardy animals are known to live more than 30 years.

EXMOOR PONY

One of the oldest English pony breeds, the Exmoor, at $12\frac{1}{2}$ hands, is an ideal saddle horse for children. It is a good jumper, is patient, and has a quiet temperament. Its lightly colored muzzle and thick, curly winter mane are common characteristics.

DARTMOOR PONY

With its rather small head, pointed ears, and powerful back, the Dartmoor is also seen as a fine pony for young riders due to its reliability and gentle temperament. Coat coloring is shades of brown. The Dartmoor is also a good jumper. Size: $12\frac{1}{4}$ hands.

WELSH MOUNTAIN PONY

This breed belongs to the class of peat bog and English mountain ponies. It has a beautiful head with large eyes and is known for its courage and endurance. Aside from its qualities as a harness horse, it is suitable as a saddle horse for children. The coloring can be of almost any shade. Size: 12 hands.

WELSH PONY

This saddle horse has an amiable character, but it can sometimes be reckless. It is an excellent jumper, an accomplished athlete with a supple gait and remarkable endurance. This breed has a variety of solid coat colors. Welsh ponies are often crossbred in order to get different sizes and types. Size: 12 to 13½ hands.

WELSH COB

This powerful and stocky horse is capable of easily jumping a small stream at full gallop. An excellent mount, it is also used for hunting, as a carriage horse, and for jumping. It has a good character and can be ridden by both children and adults. The Welsh Cob is proven to have great courage and endurance. Size: 14¾ hands.

HIGHLAND PONY

The Highland Pony, also called the Highland Carron, is a solidly built horse still used for hunting and as a pack animal in the mountainous regions of Scotland. Its gentle character makes it a remarkable saddle horse. Size: 14¼ hands.

CONNEMARA PONY

This breed is a native of Ireland. Growing up partly in the wild, it is used as a saddle horse as well as in sports, such as polo. It has a good character, a quiet temperament and is a good jumper. Many Connemaras are grey in color. Size: 12¾ to 14 hands.

NEW FOREST PONY

These ponies live outdoors almost all year long. They have an imposing head and a rather short neck. Their character is sweet and they make good saddle ponies. The characteristics of New Forests can vary greatly, as well as their size: 11¾ to 14¼ hands.

11

Horse Breeds

ARAB

Its principal characteristics are a rather small head, very large and well–rimmed nostrils, a long arched neck, and very muscled shoulders. It has straight legs, joints well adapted for jumping, and a solid coat. The Arab is a horserac-ing favorite. Size: 14¼ to 15¼

ANGLO–ARAB

A cross between an Arab and an English thoroughbred, the stal-lion is usually Arab and the mare English. Horses resulting from this coupling grow larger than either of their parents. These are excellent saddle and jumping horses. Size: 15¼ to 16½ hands.

ENGLISH THOROUGHBRED ↑

A lively horse of great size, it can be unsuitable for some riders. Its reputation rests on its spirited-ness, its beauty, and its speed. A famous stallion called St. Simon has never lost a race. Size: 14¾ to 16¾ hands.

FRENCH TROTTER ↑

With a withers height of 16½ hands, this horse is excellent for racing, either in harness or mounted. It has a hardy constitu-tion and remarkable endurance. The breed came from Russian and American animals intro-duced to French horses.

CLEVELAND BAY

Descendant of an ancient English breed, its coat is brown with sometimes a white star on the forehead. All other markings are considered defects. Its strength allows it to pull a plow as well as a carriage. It is also used for crossbreeding with thorough-breds. Size: 16¼ hands.

FRENCH SADDLE HORSE

The size of this breed can surpass 16½ hands. The coat is generally brown or chestnut. The head is rather heavy and the neck is long and sturdy. This adaptable breed has three categories: jump-ing horses, race horses, and pleasure horses.

your left leg. Then, swing your right leg over the horse and let yourself slip into the saddle. Next, slide your right foot into the other stirrup. Finally, take hold of the pommel of the saddle and settle deep into the lower part of the saddle. Once in place, pull yourself up as much as possible, while remaining seated very straight. Your legs should be pressed against the animal and your heels should be down. If your position is correct, it should be possible to draw a vertical line from your earlobe to your heel. This is the basic position for most equestrian sports, with the exception of racing. This classical riding position is as practical as it is elegant. To dismount, follow the process in reverse order. Remove your foot from the right stirrup and shift your weight towards the left leg. Hold on to the pommel (without letting go of the reins!) and swing the right leg over the horse's back. Let yourself down gently, placing both feet on the ground at the same time.

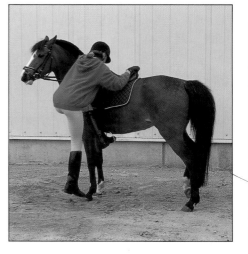

This is a bad way to dismount. For safety reasons, both feet should be together and out of the stirrups as you move to let yourself down.

Lower photo preceding page: Once in the saddle, pull yourself up as much as possible and lower your heels, holding the legs pressed against the horse's breast. When you are well placed, it should be possible to draw a vertical line from your ear to your heel. This is the classic position.

To dismount, first slip the right foot out of the stirrup and swing the right leg over the horse's back to bring it alongside the left leg. Then, slip the left foot out of the other stirrup and slowly, without rushing, let yourself down. Both feet should reach the ground at the same time.

Correct Seat

The classic position, where the rider sits very erect and with shoulders pulled back, is also often called the dressage position. Your seat is re-laxed, in the hollow of the saddle. Try to keep your shoulders parallel to those of your mount. The upper arms fall naturally, without stiffness, downwards from the shoulders, not pulled against the body or spread out like a pair of wings. If you don't sit properly, you risk having problems using the reins. The lower arm, the rein hand, and the reins should establish a straight line to the horse's mouth. The two hands should never be more than six inches (15 cm) or so apart. The reins, which must not be tangled, should pass between the last two fingers to the inner (palm side) part of the hand and come out between the thumb and index finger in the direction of the horse's neck. The thumb, which presses the reins against the index finger, will prevent slipping. The knees should be kept pressed well against the saddle. A straight line drawn from the knee to the tip of the boot should be the exact same length as the stirrup strap. Although this classic position is observed for dressage, there is a different position used for running and jumping, one designed to relieve some of the pressure on the animal's back. The difference consists in bending the upper body for-ward so that you no longer remain permanently seated in the saddle; for this position, move the hands forward on the reins and grasp them under the mane as you lean stretched over the animal's neck.

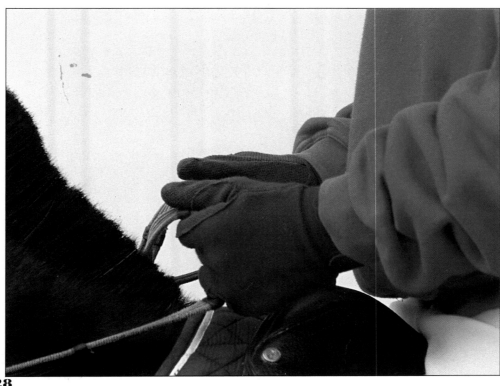

Above: Sit right in the center, not leaning to the left or right. Pull your shoulders straight back with-out dropping them. The arms hang loosely along the body.

Left: Keep your hands towards the horse's mouth. Pass the reins through the two last fingers to the inside (palm) of your hand, then out and forward from between the thumb and index finger. The wrists should remain straight, with palms facing. The forearms form a right angle with the upper arms, on a straight line with the reins. The thighs are held against the body of the horse, knees settled firmly against the saddle, and lower legs posi-tioned near the flanks.

The body of the rider is leaning too far back.

This rider's legs are too far forward.

This rider is not in correct position: it hollows out the back.

This rider is not balanced and is seated too far forward.

Correct position of the forearm: it forms an open angle with the upper arm and a straight line with the reins, in the direction of the horse's mouth.

The classic position: back straight, shoulders back and relaxed. It is possible to draw a straight vertical line linking the ear to the heel.

The correct length of the stirrup strap is determined by the distance separating the knee from the toes. The ball of the foot rests in the stirrup.

The tip of the boot is pointing up: this is the right position.

The position of the lower leg is correct if you can draw a straight line leading from the toe of the boot to the knee. This rider's lower leg is a little too far forward.

29

Riding Aids

TYPES OF AIDS

Aids are the means a rider uses to guide his horse. They are generally divided into two categories:

1. *natural aids*: the rider's body (legs, hands), seat, and voice;
2. *artificial aids*: the bridle, spurs, riding whip, and reins generally used during training; the martingale is specific to jumping hurdles.

USE OF THE AIDS

1. The reins transmit orders to the horse's mouth; they are usually used to slow or stop forward movement.
2. The legs as aids move the horse forward; encourage it to maintain or change a gait and move in rhythm.
3. Aids provided by the rider's seat, or position in the saddle, are always combined with those of the legs; they may be used to urge forward motion or to slow the horse.
4. The mount can also be influenced by the rider's voice.

The training of a horse has several advantages: it makes the animal more flexible and athletic and teaches him to obey riders who use "aids" to make their wishes known. Using seat and legs, the rider needs to be able to get the horse under him to move forward at a walk, a trot, or a canter, to stop, turn, back up, and perform other movements. Certain signals, called riding aids, are used by riders to tell the horse what to do and how to do the wanted maneuver correctly. Beginning riders often complain that their mounts don't obey them right away; often it is because the riding aids are not being used correctly. The horse doesn't understand. This is why learning the aids and how to apply them is so important. All the aids used in horseback riding are based on the horse's natural reactions; an obedient horse, then, is really doing nothing but acting naturally.

Get the feel of the horse's body rocking from left to right and try to maintain the rhythm.

With the hand holding the reins, follow the natural movement of the animal's head and nape of neck.

Support the horse's natural gait with your own legs: left, right, left, right.

FROM STANDSTILL TO WALK

The natural reaction of a horse to a change in situation is flight; so its first reaction to pressure from the legs will be a forward movement, a way to escape. Horseback riding is based on this reaction. This movement forward is the very basis of training and the use of aids. To start off, the horse must feel just enough pressure from your legs to make him leave the standing position and move forward. The pressure from both legs should be brief, not continuous, and applied just behind the cinch. At the same time, loosen your hold on the reins slightly. If your mount doesn't obey, repeat the order with a little more force, or use a riding whip to support the signal from your legs.

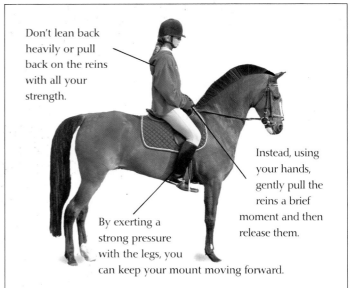

Don't lean back heavily or pull back on the reins with all your strength.

Instead, using your hands, gently pull the reins a brief moment and then release them.

By exerting a strong pressure with the legs, you can keep your mount moving forward.

STOPPING

When you wish to stop, gently contract the muscles of the lower back while pressing your lower legs against the horse's body at the height of the cinch. At the same time, alternately pull on and release the reins, and repeat the process. Although the press of your leg pushes the horse forward, your pull on the reins interrupts the rhythm of his movement forward, to the point where he stops.

THE LEFT TURN

Pull on the left rein with that hand.

Give the right rein some slack, but without losing contact with the horse's mouth.

Push the horse to the side by bringing the left leg up to the level of the cinch.

Move the right leg back a bit, to a little behind the cinch.

Shift your weight and bring the lower while bringing the of the cinch. Pull on the left rein and push the horse with the left leg. The backhand is moved towards the right; the horse turns on the forehand. slightly to the left, right leg back a bit left leg to the level

BACKING UP

Make backing up easier for your horse by pulling yourself up out of the saddle a little, making yourself lighter.

Strong pressure of your legs combined with your pull on the reins will cause the horse to begin backing up.

Much depends on the handling of the reins; the fists must be turned inward and the reins held firmly.

Contract the muscles of the lower back, then smoothly urge the horse forward with the lower legs while pulling the reins towards you.

FROM WALK TO TROT

Think of the proper seat. Contract the muscles of the lower back forcefully.

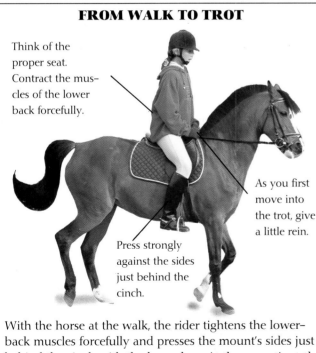

As you first move into the trot, give a little rein.

Press strongly against the sides just behind the cinch.

With the horse at the walk, the rider tightens the lower-back muscles forcefully and presses the mount's sides just behind the cinch with the lower legs. At the same time, the rider lets the reins go a little soft, until the proper movement is begun. It is easier to act on the rhythm and the gait of a horse at the trot than while it is walking.

FROM TROT TO CANTER

Don't allow yourself to fall back into the saddle at each stride like a sack of flour.

Pull on the right rein, then release it once the canter begins.

The preceding applies also here; move *with* the animal. If you are riding clockwise around the ring, the horse should move into the canter on the right (the right front leg should be the first to move forward as the leg aid is applied). Just before cornering, take your horse a bit to the right by placing your own left leg just behind the cinch and the right directly over it. Pull gently on the right rein and release, while energetically prodding with your right lower leg.

Manege Figures

Manege figures are movements designed to train the horse and develop the abilities of the rider, and are practiced to keep up the caliber of both. The execution of manege figures forces the rider to learn to use the aids perfectly. It is an ideal way for an instructor to judge a student's progress. The beginner should practice these figures in a manege ring or on a course, but also do them out of doors, where influences or distractions will need to be taken into account. There, mount and rider will often face situations that will never present them-selves in the manege, but both must be able to handle such unforeseen problems before they can be considered in control. A normal manege mea-sures 33 by 44 yards (20 by 40 m); a giant manege, 44 by 88 yards (40 by 80 m). From these dimensions, it possible to divide the manege into zones. This makes it possible to execute the different figures towards the center starting on the left hand as well as on the right. Experienced riders recognize the value of manege figures, which allow them to con-stantly refine the effectiveness of their aid use and improve the obedience of their mounts. A variety of figures are required during dressage competitions. The exercises are of no use unless they are done properly. It is from the mastery of figures in the ring that one recognizes the true horseman. The differ-ent points in a riding school ring are referred to by letters. See the letters used and their corresponding locations in these drawings.

The "change of hand" con-sists of first leading the horse from the left side through the middle of the ring to the right side.

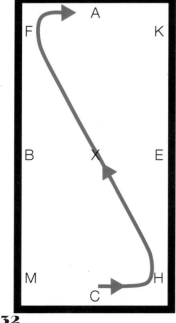

This change of hand can be done on the diagonal (left hand) as well as down the middle (or the double, big sides or small sides).

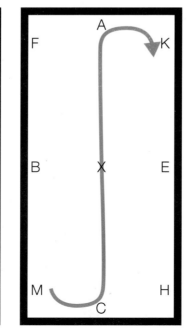

The reverse demi-volt is a demi-volt followed by an oblique line leading to the point of departure (change of hand).

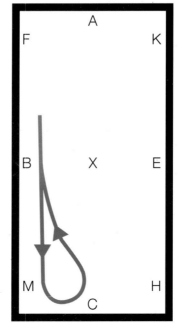

The small volt is, in fact, a complete circle on oneself. You travel a circle with about 10 feet (3 m) radius, after which you continue your course in the same direction.

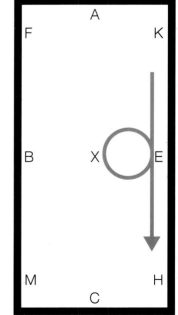

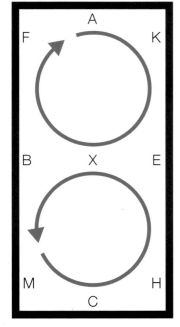

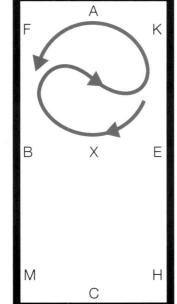

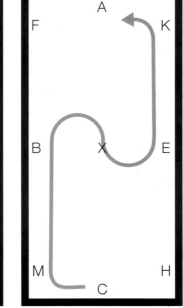

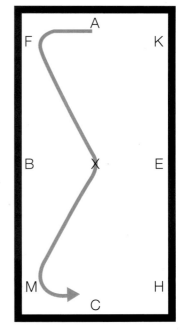

The large volt is making a loop around the entire width of the ring.

This is also a serpentine. It consists of two opposing volts and is used for the change of hands.

During the large volt, you can change hands in the form of an "S".

The broken line consists of traveling diagonally from the long side in towards the center, then moving diagonally again away towards the outside.

For the change of hands on an "S", you must drive your mount with the lower leg and the thrust of your own weight, not merely by pulling on the reins.

The double "serpentine." This is the first of a group of exercises in an adaptable series of successive turns.

The simple "serpentine." Maintain your horse's rhythm by keeping the animal well in hand and using the aids wisely.

The sinuous volt consists of a series of demi-volts. Since you must make well-drawn arcs, it is well worth shortening the inside rein.

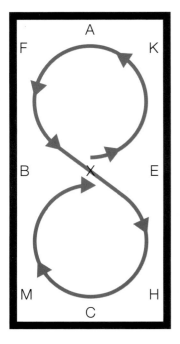

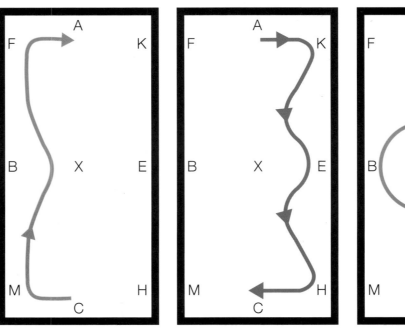

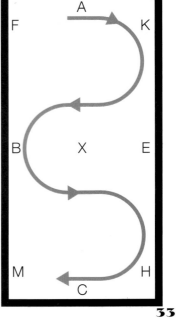

The Trot

Above: The aids used to move from walk to trot are similar to those that signal the walk. Contract the muscles of the lower back and exert strong pressure with the lower legs, while slackening the reins. Signal the start of the trot at the first stride. The horse should be into the trot by the third stride.

Horses have several ways of moving. Whether they go at a walk, a trot, or a canter or at full gallop, each movement has its own rhythm. The rider needs to vary the tempo often in order to maintain a well-marked trot. It is up to the rider to set the rhythm. The trot can be considered a two-movement gait; it can also be divided into the little trot, the working trot, and the extended trot. It is easier to vary the rhythm of a trotting horse than one that is walking; it is important to stay seated in the saddle at each stride and adapt gently to the rhythm. The beginner, however, will very likely feel shaken up and down by the rhythm of the trot. It is only when a rider is able to hold a glass of water without spilling it, with a mount trotting under him, that the gait can be considered mastered.

It's important to properly position the hands and keep your elbows against your hips. Your lower legs should neither bounce nor squeeze too much. Also, don't forget the propulsion aids during the trot. While trotting, you can either remain seated in the saddle–seated trot–or raise yourself up and reseat yourself in rhythm with the movement–called posting the trot.

Above: The lower leg rests quietly against the horse. Once you feel the tempo weaken, increase the pressure. Gently bring the outside leg behind the cinch, while the other remains active at the level of the cinch.

Right: The trot moves more easily if, rather than remaining seated, you raise up in the saddle slightly at the first stride and sit back down at the second, called posting, Once you achieve this one-two, up-down movement, you will see how helpful it is. Try to get totally into the rhythm by counting to yourself: one-two, one-two.

34

It is by remaining in the saddle, very straight but supple, that the rider's center of gravity can be found where it belongs, over that of the horse.

The hands are held vertically, thumbs up and pinkies turned inward towards the navel, without stiffness about 4 inches (10 cm) above the saddle.

The knees touch the saddle but without squeezing too much; the lower legs hang loosely but in contact with the breast.

SEATED TROT

This is what it is called when the rider stays seated on every stride. It is the opposite of the posting, or raised, trot. The first concern is to learn proper balance during the horse's movements. Also, from the beginning, you must try to remain flexible, yielding to the motions and remaining seated and in contact with the saddle on each stride. At first, you will probably find yourself being bounced from one side to the other, but after some training you will soon overcome this problem, too. Remember not to sit stiffly in the saddle; on the contrary, relax. Try to feel the rhythm of the trot, keeping your elbows close to your hips and your hands in place.

FROM TROT TO WALK

By contracting the muscles of your lower back, exerting pressure with both lower legs against the cinch, and alternately pulling on and releasing the reins, your horse will move from the trot to the walk. This is how to come to a gradual stop. With the signal completed, the horse comes to a full halt.

35

The Canter

The canter, also called the slow gallop, is generally a more enjoyable gait than the trot. Although the pace is faster, the seat is easier. Here too, however, you should not sit stiffly; if you fall back heavily on the saddle after each stride, the horse will lose its

This incorrect position must be avoided during the canter: leaning forward over the horse's neck.

smooth gait. During the canter, bring one of your legs more forward than the one on the other side; the rider decides which leg will furnish this extra lateral support. If is the right leg, it is called a right–hand canter; if the reverse, it is a left–hand canter.

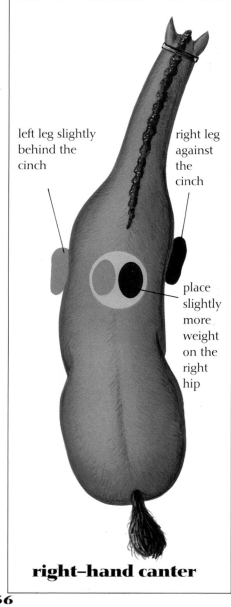

left leg slightly behind the cinch

right leg against the cinch

place slightly more weight on the right hip

right–hand canter

Another error is hollowing the back: sitting too far forward in the saddle. This position lowers the flexibility of the shoulders and arms and makes you lose contact with the horse's mouth. It also prevents you from adapting properly to your horse's moves, weakening your seat and causing a feeling of insecurity.

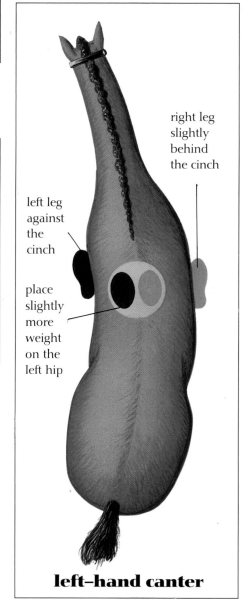

right leg slightly behind the cinch

left leg against the cinch

place slightly more weight on the left hip

left–hand canter

The canter is a gait where all four legs leave the ground at the same time at a precise moment. The horse here is in a right-hand canter; that is, his right legs—front and back—are directing his gait. In this case, the four legs move in the following order: rear left, rear right, front left, and front right.

In order to keep proper balance at the canter, a horse in a ring should be able to run in such a way that the legs on the inward side provide most of the push forward. This is especially important at the turns. In the ring, the legs on the right side are more important if he is running right-handed and the other way if he is going left-handed. The horse must always be signaled in advance of pushing him to a canter; if he is to go to the right, then it is from this side that you must put him into position and place your own outer leg—the left one—a little behind, with the right remaining pressed against the cinch. Then, gently pull the inside rein, while holding the other firmly so that the horse will not shy toward the inside of the ring. At the moment when you push him to the canter, release the inside rein slightly. If he takes the reverse canter, it means that the reins are reversed.

The signal to canter comes, first, from the forward push of your iliac bone with the contraction of the muscles of the lower back. The use of the lower-back aids alone are useless without those of the legs.

With the aid of your lower legs, push the horse forward, the inside leg at the level of the cinch, the other a little behind.

To maintain the canter and avoid the horse's return to the trot, the seat is very important. Be sure to position the inside hip slightly forward and the outside leg slightly back. Also, hold the outside rein firmly while alternately releasing and pulling on the inside rein in the rhythm of the canter.

37

Jumping

Posting trot

You can get your horse over small hurdles like the cavaletti by raising yourself up slightly in the saddle. It is important, here, to squeeze with your knees at the last stride of the gallop before reaching the hurdle. The stirrups are two holes higher.

Jump bars

At first, the horse learns to simply step over bars placed on the ground at the walk and the trot; this reinforces self-confidence. The distance between the bars depends on the horse's stride.

Jumping cavaletti

Cavaletti are long bars placed at a height of about 8 inches (20 cm). When in motion, the horse is forced to raise his feet higher than usual. Clearing the cavaletti is done at both the walk and the trot.

One fine day you will see, positioned in the training ring, one or two poles painted red and white and you will hear whispers: "We're going to jump." This time, after warming up the horse, you take up the stirrups two little holes.

Just as with the trot, when you jump you need to get used to some new moves. But, after a while, you will fall into all these movements automatically.

The first hurdles you will have to clear will likely be about 24 to 32 inches (60 to 80 cm) high. During competition, the bars can be raised to about 5 to 5½ feet (1.5 to 1.7 m). Two important jumping terms are the take-off and the landing. In both cases, it is most important that the rider stay with the horse's movement. During the take-off, the speed of the horse will increase sharply; and, at the same time, the horizontal forward movement of the front legs will change into an upward thrust forward.

Once you are used to being around horses and you feel confident, you can try a few basic techniques such as going over low hurdles by stepping over them and by jumping them. For a horse beginning to jump, however, even a small hurdle can seem difficult.

Comes the moment of your first jump. During the run to the hurdle, you must steady yourself in the saddle and direct the horse towards the hurdle as if it didn't exist. Then you must allow the horse to handle on his own his last two strides before the jump. He will select the best hoof positions based on his rhythm and should not be distracted. When the horse takes off, the rider rises up in the saddle and leans forward. Supporting his arms on the animal's neck, the rider energetically squeezes with his knees. During the jump, the horse stretches its head and neck forward; the rider's hands should go along with this movement up to the furthest stretch of the neck. At the landing, you need to gently return to the saddle and not remain hanging on your mount's neck.

This is why it is important that a rider's center of gravity shifts forward. To do this, the rider stands up slightly in the saddle and leans the upper body far forward. During the jump, his position is firm thanks to the tight pressure of the knees against the saddle; if necessary, the rider can hang on to the mane. If, on the other hand, a rider hangs on to the saddle, his center of gravity moves backwards and can cause him to fall at the end of the jump. At the moment of landing, the rider needs to use the knees as shock absorbers. The arms can also play this role when a rider, at this moment, briefly supports himself on the horse's neck. The return to the saddle must be done gently; if a rider falls back heavily after each jump, his mount will quickly lose any taste for jumping. The first hurdle is usually placed in the middle of the long side, so you jump it either left- or right-handed. Often, the horse is walked up to this first hurdle so the animal can take the time to see that it is nothing to fear as insurmountable.

Move the center of gravity forward. The arms remain bent, the hands against the horse's neck.

The rider must look for an alternative support; this is provided by maximum pressure of the knees against the saddle.

The stirrup strap has been shortened. The feet are thrust into the stirrups up to the ankle, toes turned upward.

39

Working on the Longe

Lessons on the longe, a long tether or rein, is excellent practice for maintaining balance or correcting the seat.

Longe exercises offer numerous advantages. The instructor can devote more attention to the student and the beginning rider can concentrate better, confident that the instructor is keeping the horse under control. The longe movement, in circles, is also better for improving balance or seat than straight–line movement. Freed also of coping with stirrups and reins, the rider automatically looks for support in an optimal seat. Exercises on the longe are a "must" for beginners, but are also useful to more advanced riders. Most riders have some bad habits and, by working on the longe under the direction of a good instructor, these are corrected more quickly. This type of practice on a young horse will teach a new mount to obey a rider's voice and to adjust his muscles to take the rider's weight. The longe is attached to a ring on a special halter called a curb. The horse is forced to do exercises at a walk and at a trot, left–handed as well as right–handed.

Work on hurdles, while on the longe, is practiced in a similar manner, except that the circle the horse makes on the longe should not be too small. The curb and the other parts of the harness should fit the animal well and the length of the longe line should stay the same throughout the exercise.

When a horse works on the longe, on a seating or mounted gymnastics exercise for example, it is possible to use backup accessories that prevent him from freely moving his head and neck. This is not something to worry about. On the contrary, the animal will not only be calmer, but will move more regularly during the workout, which can be very helpful to new riders having their first lessons. If schooling on the longe is sufficiently advanced, you can try mounting your horse during the course of an exercise.

The curb is often used when working young horses on the longe, those that may not yet be used to the bit. It is easier to direct such an animal in a circle with the curb, rather than the possibly frightening sudden action of a bit in his mouth. Work on the longe should be alternated between left–handed and right–handed exercises and at the three basic gaits: walk, trot, and canter; this last should not be practiced until the animal has appropriately completed his schooling in the two other gaits.

Trail Riding

When beginning riders have had enough basic instruction and are ready, the instructor will lead them on a ride outdoors. Rambling through woods and fields is very relaxing, and there is a feeling of freedom of movement and total contact with nature; this, by the way, is also the way the horse feels. If daily lessons and training have been the main part of his life up until now, this being out of doors almost totally changes things: the horse will feel a crazy desire to stretch his legs. While the manege ring represents routine, here it is relaxation: the horse sees, hears, and smells all kinds of things which can make him curious, distracted, or even reckless. A reflection in low light, a sudden gust of wind, these things will cause a horse to react according to his character, his age, and his breed. A horse may concentrate on his footing in order not to stumble, or he may find a wide sandy road a good occasion for a fast gallop To face up to such challenges, a rider will need more than a firm seat; this is why a rider needs to be able to move a horse from one gait to a slower one. Never let a horse canter if you are not sure you can stop him without difficulty, especially an all-out gallop—however beautiful, level, and inviting the road. Many accidents could be avoided if riders would conform to such safety rules. If you love horses, you need to behave responsibly, because to the animal you are master.

Nature is constantly providing new and interesting things to distract or excite a horse, so a rider must be ready for any reaction. Knowing about the natural behavior of horses will allow a rider to "see the danger coming" and prevent accidents.

Unless your horse really knows a route, you can't simply ride and not be alert to your horse and surroundings. Guide him calmly, in a disciplined manner, holding a straight line. Be careful in traffic and signal him, when to slow down.

The pasture is the best place to prepare for riding in the country. Shorten the stirrup straps one or two holes. The basic exercises consist of practicing the walk, using longer reins, in position to change to a canter.

In some countries, the minimum age for riding a horse on public roads is twelve years. Always obey traffic laws and, for safety, try to ride in a group led by a riding instructor, even if you are an accomplished rider. Never forget that your horse is an animal, and understands nothing of modern traffic. You need to be responsible for your mount as well as yourself.

Buying a Horse or Pony

If you are crazy about horses and are interested in a particular equestrian sport, you may be thinking about buying your own horse. Before you decide, there are a whole series of things to take into consideration. Price is, of course, one concern in this type of acquisition, but there is also the level of experience and technical capability of the rider. While an accomplished rider may feel comfortable negotiating the purchase of an animal that has not yet been broken, intending to train it personally, the beginner should select an older horse, one that is more stable and well broken in. Older riders should avoid buying a young, high-spirited animal, where there is more risk of taking a bad spill; for them, falling can have many more consequences than for the young. The basic rule is to not overestimate your own capabilities. Another matter to consider: for complete harmony, the size and weight of a horse should always be in relation to those of the rider. The breed and coat color are of minor importance in buying a horse; the most essential points are the health and obedience of the animal. The price of a horse is generally dependent on age, performance, general look, and state of health. The origins and size also frequently enter into account, especially with regard to race horses. Finally, you must really think about whether you have the time to devote to your horse and if you can offer him decent shelter. When it appears that you can satisfy all these conditions, what else remains to be considered?

Before buying "your heart's desire" you had best examine him from top to bottom. Make sure that he eats willingly and well and benefits from it: you wouldn't want to find yourself with an animal who eats

If you want to acquire a certain horse, you first need to get to know him. You can, for example, go and take him out of the stable on your own to observe his reactions: Does he seem gentle or does he immediately run to the farthest corner when you near the door? The horse you buy should be agreeable and cooperative towards his future owner; you will be spending many hours together and will want to establish a climate of mutual friendliness and confidence.

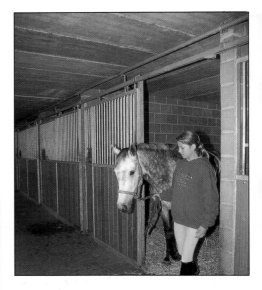

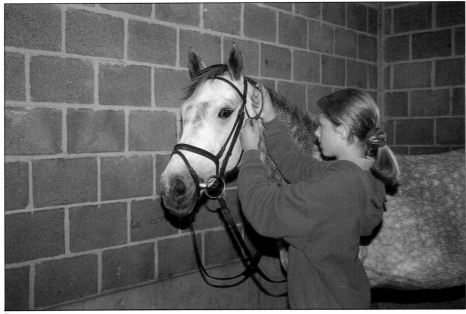

Before buying a horse, make sure that he will let himself be groomed without fuss, that he is not inclined to bite, is attentive to the aids, etc. Ask the owner if you can go around the manege a few times, and then test a possible candidate at the walk, the trot, and the canter. If, at this stage, you still like the horse but his health remains a question, ask a veterinarian to examine him. Obviously, this will not be free, but it's best to pay such fees and be completely assured that your new friend is in good health and perfect shape.

Right: Horses and ponies are used more and more for sports activities and leisure. It's possible to go riding in all seasons as long as the animal is in good health and the rider is equipped to function in the existing conditions. Whether the activity lasts an hour, a day, or longer depends on the physical condition of the horse and the experience of the rider.

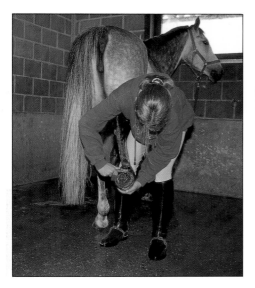

Above: Grooming is one of the daily chores of the horse lover; through this process, the animal remains in good condition and the circulation of blood to the skin is intensified. The hoof pick is used to rid the hooves of pebbles and other foreign bodies; a damaged hoof can easily become infected and cause limping.

large amounts but still looks like skin and bones. What do the hooves look like? Will you have to change the shoes often, or are the hooves sturdy and healthy? To be sure, it is important to ride the animal unshod as well. Another important point: how does the horse respond when you harness him? Can you take hold of his feet without a problem? How does he behave in the stable? Don't forget to ask about possible lesions of the genitalia. If everything seems positive, you should finally let him run without either rider or saddle and watch him attentively. Then ask that someone ride him by you while you watch. And, finally and obviously, ride him yourself.

One last word: Horses are, by nature, gregarious. This means that they need company to be happy. The horse who spends all day alone in his stable will turn sour-tempered and become unsociable. If you don't have the money or room for a second horse (or a pony), plan to get a couple of other domestic animals to keep your horse company.

Right: If you believe that your horse has some problem or other, don't hesitate to call the veterinarian; it is up to an expert to examine him, not the master. Even well-cared-for horses can get sick; they are very sensitive to certain diseases and viruses. Horses must be vaccinated against ailments such as tetanus and the flu, and the veterinarian must take care of giving these shots. Horses also often suffer from worms. Without adequate treatment, the consequences can be serious; but a vermifuge can avoid such problems.

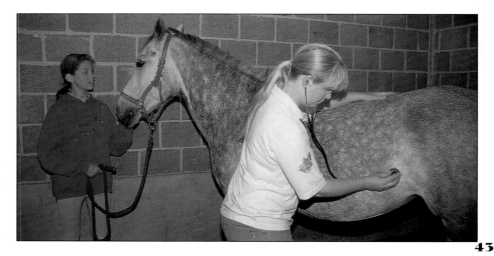

Horsemanship Terms

AIDS: devices available to the rider in guiding a mount:

>**natural aids:** seat, legs, hands, voice

>**artificial aids:** reins, spurs, riding whip, bit, etc.

BACKHAND: rear part of the horse, comprising the croup and the rear limbs, situated "behind the hand" of the rider

BAY: a reddish-brown coat coloring, with black mane and extremities

BIT: a metal mouthpiece, attached to the bridle, which is placed in the horse's mouth

BRIDLE: a light harness with a broken bit

BROWBAND: the part of the harness that goes over the horse's forehead

CANTER: the fastest of three training gaits, this three-beat gait is also called slow gallop

CANTLE: the rear part of the saddle

CAVALETTI: long painted bars positioned about 8 inches (20 cm) above the ground, they serve as low hurdles for horses

CHANGE OF HANDS: execution of a turn going to the opposite side through the center of the ring

CHESTNUT: a reddish-yellow coat coloring and mane

CINCH: the girth strap that passes under the horse's belly and fixes the saddle in place

CINCH BUCKLE: one of the straps at the bottom of the saddle to which the main cinch is attached

COAT: a horse's fur covering, usually seen as its color

CURB: metal semicircle attached to the noseband for work on the longe

CURRYCOMB: a grooming aid used to rid a horse's coat of dirt

DAPPLED: having a spotted coat of mixed grey and white

DRESSAGE: training a horse to follow aids and do what a rider expects of him

DRESSAGE EVENT: competitions used to determine the abilities of riders in completing figures

DUN: a light yellow-brown coat coloring

FETLOCK: a tuft of hair at the back part of the horse's foot

FOAL: a baby horse, male or female (up to thirty months)

FOREHAND: the forward part of the horse, comprising the head, neck, chest, and the front limbs

GAITS: the three modes of movement of a horse, characterized by different speeds and especially different rhythms

GALLOP: when slow, also called the canter; a fast gallop has the same rhythm

GROOMING: cleaning and otherwise tending to a horse, particularly the coat

HALTER: the part of the harness placed on the horse's head in order to guide or secure him

HAND: a unit of measurement in referring to the height of horses at the withers; one hand equal to 4 inches or 10.2 centimeters.

HARNESS: reins and other gear designed for leading or working with a horse

HEADSTALL: the part of the bridle that goes over horse's head, made up of the crownpiece, browband, and noseband

HEEL: the ends of the horseshoe, extending towards the back of the foot

HOOF PICK: a metal tool for cleaning hooves

IBLIAC BONE: each of two bones which, with the sacrum, form the pelvis

LEFT HAND: the left side when looking toward the center of the ring

LEG: the stiff and elongated part of the riding boot

LEVADE: the horse's performance of rearing up on the hind legs at the command of the rider

LONGE: a long strap attached to horse's halter in order to direct him in a circular movement

MARTINGALE: a special strap that allows a rider to control a mount's head and neck movements

MOUNT: an animal ridden for transportation purposes; used here, the horse or pony

MOUNTED GYMNASTICS: gymnastic or acrobatic exercises performed while on horseback, with the mount standing still or in motion.

NECK: the part of the horse's body stretching between the head and the withers, the shoulders and the breast

NOSEBAND: the part of the harness around the lower head that prevents the horse from opening its mouth

PIROUETTE: a volt made in place by pivoting on one rear foot

PONY: an equine breed growing no taller than 14¾ hands (59 inches/147 centimeters) at the withers

POSTING (RAISED) TROT: trot during which the rider alternately raises himself up and lowers himself following the gait's cadence

REINS: straps attached to the bit that are used to guide the mount

RIDING HAT: stiff, semi–spherical headwear, worn as protection in case of falls

RIDING WHIP: a flexible rod, often called a crop, often ending in a tuft (cracker), used as an aid by riders

RIGHT HAND: the right side when looking toward the center of the ring

RING FIGURES: traditional movements of the equestrian art to be correctly executed in competition

ROAN: a coat coloring made up of mixed white, chestnut, and black hairs

SADDLE: a curved, leather device positioned on an animal's back as a seat for riding

SADDLE BOW: the stiff framework of the saddle

SEAT: the position in which a rider is seated on horseback

SEATED TROT: trot during which the rider remains seated in the saddle

SHOD: having horseshoes on the hooves

SLIPKNOT: a special knot that unties easily when the rope is pulled

SNAFFLE: a type of flexible bit

SPUR: a metal aid attached to the boot's heel, designed to goad a horse into moving forward

STIRRUP: a metal ring with a flat base, it provides support for the rider's foot

STIRRUP LEATHER: a strap to which the stirrup is attached

STRAP: a straight band of tough, flexible material, often of leather, used to link or attach; includes such things as stirrup leather, halter, longe, tether, tug chain, reins, belly band

THOROUGHBRED: a type of horse, a cross between an Arab horse and a western breed

THROATLATCH: the part of the bridle that passes under the horse's throat

TRAVOIS: a load-carrying device or stretcher made from two long branches or poles and dragged behind a horse

TROT: a faster two-beat gait

VOLT: a complete circle made on horseback; in ring figures, often 20 feet (6 m) in diameter

WALK: a slow gait; the successive placement of each leg of the horse provides a four–beat rhythm

WITHERS: the area at the top of the horse's shoulder from which we measure its height

Index

Photos: Diapress, Hippo Foto, Hans Reinhard, Bruce Coleman, Kit Houghton, Robert Harding.

Drawings: Karel Boumans.
With thanks to Hippo Shop Zoersel for valuable advice and the documentation provided for this work.

TRAKEHNER

The Trakehner, an old and fiery breed, is a native of Germany. Serving as saddle horses, they are known for their courage and stamina. Their dependable character and their temperament, so full of life, make them particularly suitable for dressage and jumping. Trakehner stallions are sought by many breeders looking to improve local, native breeds. Size: 15¾ to 16¾ hands.

HANOVER ↑

Hanovers are among the top race horses. At stud farms, a couple of hundred stallions may go through appropriate training, and scheduled public demonstrations of their talents last for two or more hours. This horse is used not only for sport, but in farming. It has a good character and is gifted in dressage. Size: 16 to 17 hands.

HACKNEY

Since its appearance, this elegant but small horse has played an important role and been much appreciated as a mode of travel because of its speed. Currently, the Hackney, with its contours and, well-proportioned gait, is in high demand for horse shows and, in harness, as carriage horse. Its coat coloring can run from brown to black. Size: 14 to 15¾ hands.

QUARTER HORSE

This American sprinter is strong and fast. It is also manageable, having been used early on for herding and in rodeos. Its friendly and calm character make it both a mount for shows and an agreeable partner for relaxing rides. Size: 14¾ to 16 hands.

ANDALUSIAN

This legendary Spanish breed is, at the present time, just as pure as it was five centuries ago. The credit for this feat goes to Carthusian monks. This magnificent mount unites strength with intelligence and elegance. Size: 16 hands.

FRIESIAN

This is the only Dutch breed whose genes have been kept pure for more than a century. Manageable horses with excellent character, they are especially coveted for the role of pleasure horse as well as for pulling loads. Size: 15 to 15¾ hands.

13

The Conformation of the Horse

The horse's form depends in large part on its breed and is an important key to choosing how the animal will be used. Horses and ponies have very straight backs, a beautiful head with brilliant and clear eyes, and a neck that extends out of well–formed shoulders; a solid chest; imposing haunches, joints well adapted for jumping, and sturdy hooves. It is the height at the withers that determines the category of horse or pony: animals growing to less than 14½ hands high at the withers are called ponies. A hand, equal to 4 inches (10.16 cm), is the standard term of measurement for horses. A draft horse should have straighter shoulders than a saddle horse. In the saddle horse, the shoulders and neck are more elongated and the feet should not come up too high off the ground in skimming gaits, notably at the trot. At this gait a draft horse, the Hackney for example, will bend more at the knee. The movements of a Moorland pony may seem unsteady, but they are important to the pony's making its way through marshy ter–rain. A stallion should have a masculine bearing and its head should express its strong charac-

ter. Its neck should be large and muscular, while that of a mare will be lighter. She should have a well–developed belly and a kind–looking face.

With its size, strength, beautiful head, and harmo-niously built body, the horse is a noble creature.

Ponies are powerful animals with a stocky build and strong limbs. England counts at least nine pony breeds. *Below:* There are many dif–ferent types of ponies.

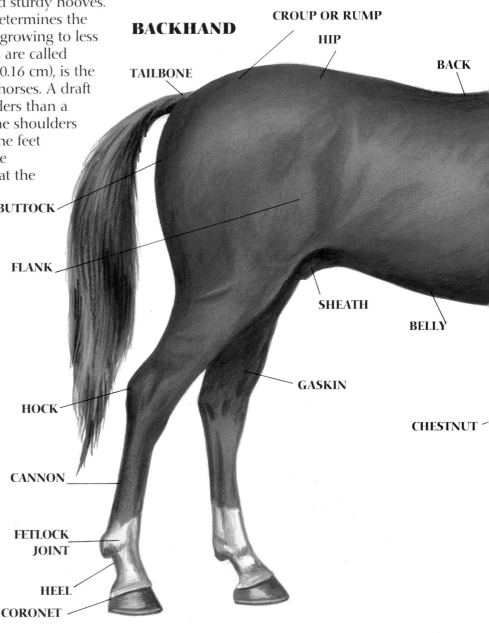

BACKHAND

CROUP OR RUMP

HIP

BACK

TAILBONE

BUTTOCK

FLANK

HOCK

CANNON

FETLOCK JOINT

HEEL

CORONET

SHEATH

BELLY

GASKIN

CHESTNUT

FOREHAND

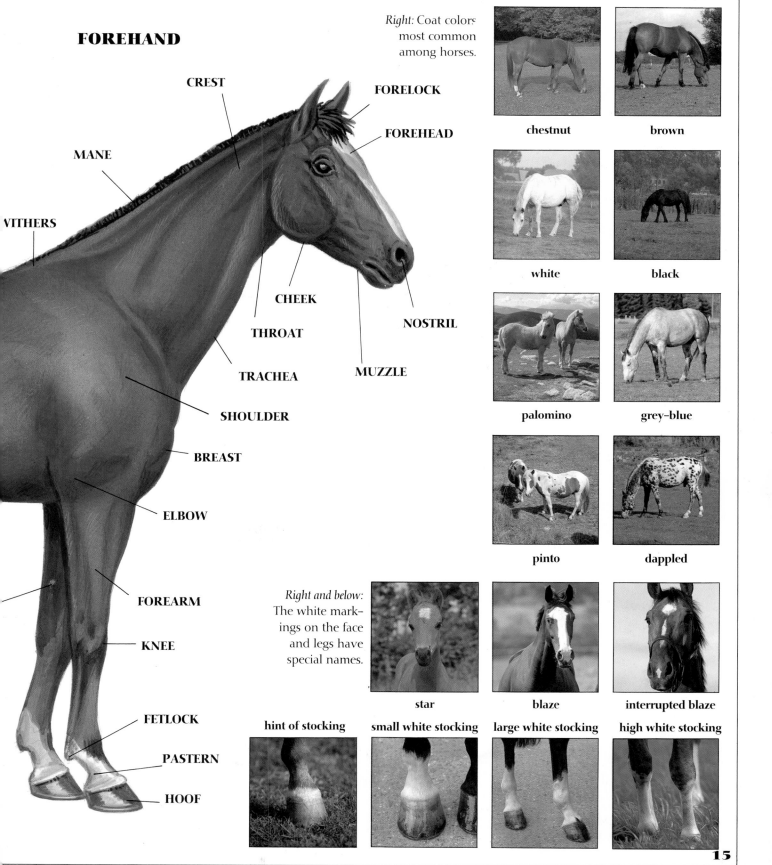

CREST

FORELOCK

FOREHEAD

MANE

VITHERS

CHEEK

THROAT

NOSTRIL

TRACHEA

MUZZLE

SHOULDER

BREAST

ELBOW

FOREARM

KNEE

FETLOCK

PASTERN

HOOF

Right: Coat colors most common among horses.

chestnut

brown

white

black

palomino

grey–blue

pinto

dappled

Right and below: The white mark–ings on the face and legs have special names.

star

blaze

interrupted blaze

hint of stocking

small white stocking

large white stocking

high white stocking

15

Quartering • The Stable • Feeding

Above: For his daily ration of exercise, fresh air, and food, a horse should ideally spend at least a couple of hours in the pasture. This practice is good for his health and also serves to lighten stable work.

Below: Only horses that have a chance to work off physical energy through a variety of daily activities should be quartered in stalls.

Below: Also, while in boxes, horses should be able to see each other and so maintain contact with stablemates.

Right: To maintain the stable properly, you will need a pitchfork for the manure, a large and sturdy broom, a rake, and a watering hose. In addition, a wheelbarrow or easy-handling gardening cart is needed to transport manure and straw.

A horse eats all day long because its stomach is not very large. In the wild, the horse must always be ready to run away quickly, so it eats only in small amounts; it would be hard to escape from danger on a full stomach. Horses that spend all their time in the pasture develop natural eating habits. If they are pastured only occasionally, they will sometimes overeat. Horses in the stable should have the benefit of three meals a day. Race horses are sometimes even given five to seven light rations a day; the more small meals they have, the better their condition. On your first daily visit to the stable, in the

Stable manure should be cleaned out daily, using a pitchfork and broom, and piled elsewhere for disposal. Larger amounts can be sold to a truck farm or gardener to be used as fertilizer. Once a week, all straw should be removed from the stable and the quarters carefully washed down with a watering hose before replacing it with fresh straw. Don't forget to wear your boots for this job.

morning, begin by giving your animal some hay: this has a calming effect since it takes time for this food to be properly chewed. Thirty to forty-five minutes later, you can provide a more concentrated food, one that the horse will eat more quickly. Oats are the horse's most important grain; it contains all the nutrients

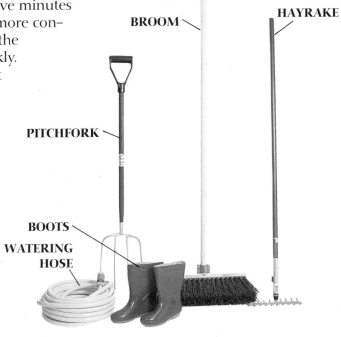

BROOM

HAYRAKE

PITCHFORK

BOOTS

WATERING HOSE

dry feed　　**oats**　　**barley**　　**mixed feed**　　**bran**

grass　　**straw**　　**hay**　　**salt block**

Make sure to vary your horse's diet. Don't give him too much oats if the work to be done is not too demanding. The salt block contains invaluable minerals for health.

Offer a treat?

A horse can lose up to 2 ounces (60 g) of salt a day from sweating. This is why the salt block is so important, it's the best way to restore lost salt. If the block is hung some-where within reach, the animal will be able to get what salt he needs from it. As a reward, when he comes readily to you or does something you have asked him to do, you can give your horse an apple, a carrot, or a piece of beet. He will enjoy and look forward to these treats. Occasionally, a piece of sugar or crust of dry bread will also be welcome. It's possible, too, to buy specially prepared treats to reward your horse.

necessary to tone the muscles and provide strength and endurance. Follow these rules at mealtimes: 1. Give some-thing to drink before giving something to eat. 2. Give little to eat, but often. 3. Don't skimp on hay, especially in the evening. 4. Don't change the type of food suddenly. 5. Keep regular meal times. 6. Don't provide food just before or after exhausting work. 7. Get good-quality feed.

Horses are generally quartered in a stable, which involves a lot of upkeep. The box dimensions should be at least 12 feet (3.65 m) square. Rye straw is good as litter or bedding as it absorbs moisture well and is longer-lasting, but you can also use sawdust and wood chips, which are a better buy.

HARMFUL PLANTS

In nature, plants can be a danger to horses and ponies. All riders should be familiar with the plants in their area, which ones are dangerous and what they look like. Serious poisoning can cause not only stomach or intesti-nal upset, but staggering or other movement problems, even paralysis. It is particu-larly important to avoid ragwort; if you find this plant anywhere, pull it up immediately, root and all, and burn it.

Yew　　**Privet**　　**Deadly Nightshade**　　**Laburnum**　　**Black Henbane**

Foxglove　　**Celandine**　　**Beech**　　**Meadow Saffron**　　**Lily of the Valley**

Getting to Know Your Horse

Horses learn from experience and in small stages. To teach them something, you need to start simple. A young animal should become accustomed as soon as possible to the halter, which will allow him to be guided and controlled. You need to gain the horse's trust and confidence by, among other things, generously rewarding him when he has earned it. This bond can be developed, too, by offering a tidbit when you are walking towards him. To more easily move the animal out of the pasture, for example,

bring with you a container holding some small treat. Approaching calmly from the front, offer him a taste. Then, carefully slip the halter over his head and lead him from the meadow. He will soon understand that he will receive the rest of the treat later and, in the future, he will allow himself to be led more easily. It is completely normal for a horse not to want to leave the pasture. He knows that he's going to have to work, carry a rider or pull a carriage,

Make sure that the halter fits properly and is in good condition. Some halters are adjustable.

Left: No horse enjoying the freedom of the pasture will easily let himself be caught, but with patience you will win over even the most stubborn.

Below: When you lead a horse to the stable, it is best to go inside with him and to close the door before letting him loose. If you undo the lead too soon, you run the risk of his taking off. In the morning, when you take him out of the stable, don't mount him right away: first give him something to eat. After his meal, the horse should have the benefit of a few hours' rest. Then, put on the halter and groom him according to your schedule. It's best to tie him during this procedure. Once the grooming is over, saddle and harness him and you will both finally be ready for an enjoyable ride.

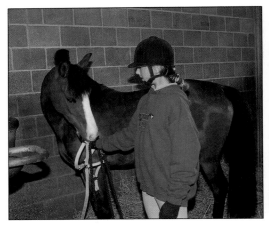

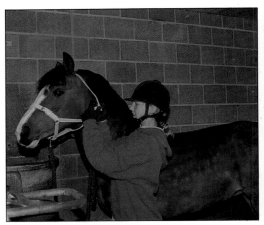

Above: Slip the throatlatch over the neck and then the noseband over the nostrils.

instead of being able to graze, lie down, or romp or run as he pleases. Some horses will go so far as to gallop to the opposite end of their field as soon as they see you coming. Such horses have undoubtedly had bad experiences with their riders or other people and no longer trust humans. If your horse behaves like that, you will have to reestablish a climate of mutual understanding with him. To do this you will need a lot of patience. Horses are, by nature, mistrustful and always remain on their guard; they abandon this attitude only very gradually, sometimes only after several weeks. Even so, a sudden movement can sometimes be misinterpreted. Don't jerk your hands around rapidly while standing close to horses, and never shout near them. A good way to quickly gain your mount's confidence is first to go, armed with a juicy reward, and find him in the pasture; then tie him near his stable using a harness and groom him from top to bottom, talking gently to him all the while. Having completed this work, give him one last reward and take him back to the pasture. In this

way, your horse will associate you with pleasure and kindness. After several days of this getting–to–know–you treatment, you can mount him for a quarter of an hour after grooming and then take him back to the field with one last reward.

Hold the loose reins in your hand, don't loop them around your hand or arm. Another tip: when leading a horse, walk alongside the horse's head at a distance of about an arm's length. This will allow you good control of the situation.

How to tie up your horse

When you have to secure an animal, make sure that the line is long enough to allow him to turn his head. This will reassure him. On the other hand, the line must not be so long that it could entangle his legs. The four–part illustration at left shows you how to easily tie up a horse using a slipknot.

Below: How to make a slipknot with the harness rope.

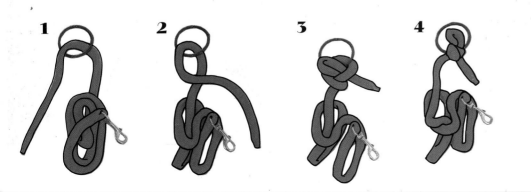

19

Grooming: Cleaning and Care

Proper grooming and brushing is important to the health of your horse. It keeps his coat in good condition, is an aid to good blood circulation, and gets rid of certain parasites. To do a good job, you need: a hard horse brush (or wisp), a currying comb, a soft brush, another brush and a hoof pick for the hooves, hoof grease, a mane comb, two or three sponges, and a woolen rag. First, use a hoof pick to remove any mud or gravel encrusted there or in and around the shoes. Work from back to front; that is, heel to toe. Begin grooming the coat by using your hand to brush off any loose dirt; then, with the hard brush, start brushing on the animal's left, moving it back and forth, front to back, and cleaning the brush regularly by knocking it against a hard, moist floor. If the hair is long and there is a lot of caked mud, you can also use a rubber currying comb. Pay special attention to places where the coat is matted. When you have finished with the two flanks, brush the mane up away from the neck and make especially sure that the neck is clean. Then let the mane fall back down naturally.

A rider should check the condition of his horse on returning from any exercise. If the legs are swollen or hot, the horse will need a treatment of cool running water. Let the water run over the legs continuously, but be sure that the pressure is not too high.

Brushes, sponges, a currying comb, and a hoof pick are some of the grooming aids for caring for your horse.

You can keep the soft brush in good shape by combing it out with the currying comb. When the body, the legs, and the mane are completely clean, go on to the head. To groom the head, you will need to undo the halter. For the moment you can fasten the halter around the horse's neck, but remember to reattach the halter once you have finished the head. One sponge should be used to clean the eyes and the nostrils, and another for the genital area. Remove knots in the tail by separating it into small tufts and brushing them from top to bottom. Clean the hooves by using the appropriate hoof pick and brush; once this is done, you can make the hooves look nicer by rubbing them with hoof grease. This practice will also prevent the hooves from drying out. For the final, finishing touch, bring out the coat's natural shine by rubbing it with a woolen rag. Your horse will look dazzling and a picture of health.

THE EYES

For the care of the eyes, you must use a clean sponge. After wringing it out, hold the horse's head with one hand while you wipe its eyes with the other.

THE MANE

First, brush the hair upwards, against the grain, then clean it thoroughly and finally let it fall back naturally.

THE SKIN

Horses may have hair that bristles, or stands erect, in cold weather, and provides better insulation. This is why, after exercising the animal and it is dry, you should use a brush to remove patches of dried sweat. The matted-down hair will then be able to stand up again and insulate the horse should the need arise.

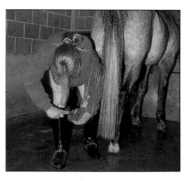

THE TAIL

Clean the tail by dividing it into small tufts and brushing each tuft from top to bottom. This way, the knots can be worked out and the tail will lay smoothly again.

PRESSURE POINTS

Even a well-placed saddle can cause sores on the withers or the back if it is not perfectly made or doesn't fit well, or if the saddle liner is folded over.

THE MUZZLE

Use a good-quality sponge to clean the nostrils, the lips, and the areas around them.

THE LEGS

Caring for the legs can take some time, since this is the part of the horse most likely to get dirty. To make the job easier, it's important to check your mount's legs as soon as your ride is over to see that mud and dirt don't cake and dry on.

UNDERSIDE OF HOOF

When cleaning out the hooves with a hoof pick, always work from the heel towards the toe, or the frontmost part of the foot. Also, check that the shoe is properly in place with no nails sticking out.

If your horse wears horseshoes, you must regularly have his hooves examined by a blacksmith. Like the nails on our fingers and toes, a horse's hooves grow. If they grow larger than the size of the shoe, they can cause the horse pain; so you will need to have the hooves filed down to size from time to time.

THE SENSITIVE AREAS

Treat your horse's sensitive areas with great care, just as you do where bones show through the skin. When you rub down these sensitive areas, you will notice the muscles contracting.

UPPER SURFACE OF HOOF

Once the hooves are brushed clean with water, they should be greased. The oil will prevent the hard surface from drying out and will give the hooves a nice appearance.

21

Riding Gear

If you are really serious about horseback riding, you will need a proper outfit. Some needed gear can seem costly, but it is usually possible to eventually find items at a better price. The various disciplines of horsemanship require specific dress. To start, comfortable slacks with a flexible lining and a pair of leather or rubber boots without laces are fine. If, later on, you are still sure about taking part in the equestrian arts, there is still time to assemble a complete wardrobe. Your first as an accomplished rider should include: 1) jodhpurs, 2) riding jacket, 3) riding boots, 4) riding hat, 5) a pair of suitable

STIRRUPS

An integral part of the saddle, the stirrups should be large and heavy to allow for an easier mount. If the horse should fall, the rider's foot should be able to slide out easily. The stirrup leathers, for safety reasons, should be made of top-quality leather. Don't use stirrups made of nickel, which are less reliable and have been known to bend or lose their shape; it's best to choose those made of stainless steel.

SADD
LININ

gloves, 6) a riding whip, and 7) your spurs, which you must first earn. Many other items will be needed to complete the list of riding gear. The bit, for example, is available in many different forms; the latest model is the snaffle bit. There are also many saddle types of varying sizes and the price can seem quite high, but if a saddle is well maintained it can last a long time. The saddle should be chosen to fit the animal well and be comfortable for the rider. Other items needed are: the cinch, the reins, the bridle, and the stirrups and stirrup leathers; here, too, you have much variety to choose from.

THE BRIDLE

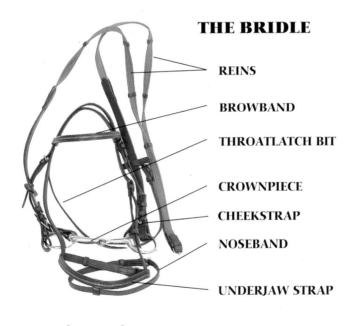

REINS

BROWBAND

THROATLATCH BIT

CROWNPIECE

CHEEKSTRAP

NOSEBAND

UNDERJAW STRAP

Needle jointed snaffle

D-ring snaffle with rollers

D-ring jointed-rubber snaffle

Chantilly or bead snaffle

Straight-rubber snaffle

Jointed snaffle with rings

SPURS: YES OR NO

Spurs should be earned: they have no place on the boots of beginners and should be awarded only after diligent training. A new rider can not use the spurs properly. You must learn first how to take a typical seat, free and supple, so you won't constantly torment a mount by repeated spurring. The spurs only serve, once you know what you are doing, to maintain a mount's rhythm. Spurs also come in different sizes and models.

WITHERS OPENING

POMMEL

CANTLE

SEAT

Left: The English saddle, the most frequently used saddle in horsemanship, is suitable for general horseback riding as well as for dressage.

JOCKEY

STIRRUP LEATHER

STIRRUP IRON

RIDING HAT
Wearing a riding hat is an important safety measure, especially during long rides and when jumping. A size that fits the wearer's skull well is an absolute necessity. A chin strap can be attached to keep the hat on securely while riding.

RIDING JACKET
This is the most popular uniform item in equestrian sports; it is very important that the fit allow the body sufficient space to move.

GLOVES
A special feature of gloves designed for riding is that they are reinforced between the thumb and the index finger and between the ring finger and the pinkie.

RIDING PANTS
Good riding pants have no seams on the inside of the thighs. At knee level on that side, pieces of leather are usually sewn on as protective padding.

RIDING BOOTS
When buying your boots, make sure that they are not only comfortable but that they are a good height for you.

THE WESTERN SADDLE
The main differences are the far-forward placement of the stirrups and the pommel mounted on the front. In the past, a saddle button behind the rider held a lasso. During the saddle's development, elements were adjusted based on the function of the horse and the rider's needs. Later, elaborate ornamentation was added.

Saddling and Harnessing

The great moment has arrived: your first outing on horseback. But first you need to saddle and harness up. This should be done with the greatest of care, as a badly adjusted saddle can be annoying or even painful to either horse and rider or prevent you from holding the correct riding position. The saddle's weight should be distributed as equally as possible over the back muscles of the horse, but it is very important to allow the horse free movement at the shoulders. The saddle should be placed while standing on the left side of the horse; it should be positioned first at the top of the withers and then slipped into its proper position to lie flat. Buckle the cinch securely to keep the saddle firmly in place.

Above left: Lightly place the reins on the horse's neck. Take the bit in your left hand, while holding the bridle with your right. Then, smoothly, place the bit in the horse's mouth.

Center left: Carefully slip the bridle over the ears and place the forelock over the browband to prevent the bridle from sliding back-wards. Be careful not to pull so tightly that you squeeze the ears.

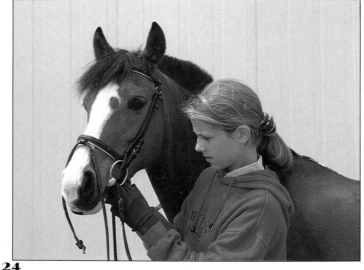

Below left: Now, look at the throat and nose bands. The throatlatch should be loose enough for you to place your fist between it and the horse's throat. The noseband should also not be too tight: you should be able to slip two fingers under it. Finally, check the position of the bit.

Below: When you take off the bridle after work, start by detaching the throat and nose bands. Then, bring the reins and throatlatch forward together over the horse's ears and let the bit slip gently out of the mouth. Gather it up with your free hand.

Put on a saddle blanket and smooth it out to the withers. This will protect the horse's skin from rubbing sores.

Then, place the saddle high on the withers and let it slide back and settle in the hollow (lowest point).

Finally, grasp the cinch with your right hand, pass it under the horse, and fasten it to the outside cinch attachments.

Every time you mount, check the tension of this cinch. If it is too loose, tighten it carefully; the strap should have enough holes to allow for correction. When you are fitting the snaffle bit, the model most recommended for beginners, make sure that the throatlatch is not too tight as this could interfere with the animal's breathing; if, on the other hand, this strap is too loose, the whole bridle could slip off the horse's head. Pass the reins up over the neck. Grasp the bit with your left hand while, with the right, you keep hold of the upper part of the head-stall; then, slip the bit into the horse's mouth and the headstall up over the ears. Make sure that no folds of skin or strands of mane are pinched and that none of the leather straps are twisted; then buckle the throatlatch securely. Now it is time to check that the noseband and the bit are correctly in place. Adjust the stirrups to the desired height. Once in the saddle, check the cinch again for safety. Often, despite everything, you have to readjust something or other.

Make sure that the cinch is not causing pressure anywhere and that it is not twisted. The strap should have a sufficient number of holes to allow for any necessary adjustment. The stirrups, which are held in place by metal hooks, should be adjusted to a length that is good for the particular rider.

Before mounting, check that:

- the cinch is securely fastened
- the saddle is properly placed
- the throatlatch is correctly tightened

Don't forget that the stirrup leathers should be pulled up as high as possible, so that the buckle will wind up being at the very top, under the jockey.

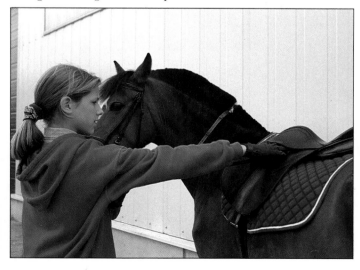

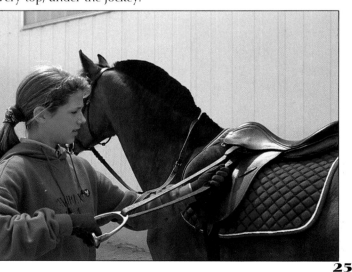

Mounting and Dismounting

There are several ways to mount a horse. The most practical and safest is to use the stirrup on the animal's left side. As you may have noticed, most actions take place on this side: putting on the saddle, adjusting the cinch, mounting, dismounting, the start of grooming, and so on. This is traditional.

Accidents while mounting are usually due to the carelessness of the rider. There are three important safety measures to keep in mind: 1) Select an adequate, relatively smooth mounting area on firm ground. 2) Check the cinch adjustment: a saddle that bounces around can make the horse anxious and throw the rider off balance. 3) If you are learning or unsure of yourself, ask someone to help you by holding the horse's head. The horse's head should remain steady and not move, first of all to avoid accidents but also as a matter of discipline for the horse from the moment the rider mounts. As you mount, face towards the rump. Take the reins in your left hand at the withers, and the stirrup in your right hand. Then, put your left foot in this stirrup. With the right hand, which is now free, grasp the saddle cantle and pull yourself up, using both arms, while pushing off strongly with

Once up, check that:

- the cinch does not have to be tightened
- stirrups are at good height

Below: Hold the saddle firmly with the left hand and the stirrup with the right hand. Put your left foot in that stirrup and grasp the saddle cantle with your right hand. Pull yourself up and swing your right leg over the horse's back. Let yourself down into the saddle and slide your right foot into the other stirrup. Settle in comfortably and correct your position.